SylvaC

A
PRICE GUIDE
to
Falcon Factory Items

Mick and Derry Collins

By the same authors:

AN INTRODUCTION TO SYLVAC

First published 1988
Revised edition 1990

COLLECTING SYLVAC

First published 1998

First published in March 1999

ISBN 0 9514202 2 4

Designed by Mick Collins and published by S.C.C. Publications, Horndean, Hants.

Printed in the U.K. by Selsey Press Ltd., 84, High Street, Selsey, Chichester, West Sussex. PO20 0QH

INTRODUCTION

(It is important to read this section to obtain an understanding of the confusing Shaw and Copestake mould numbering system).

The mould numbering system used by Shaw and Copestake (SylvaC) for their products has led to much bewilderment amongst collectors, due mainly to the usage of the same set of numbers twice, i.e. the numbers 1 to 759. We hope that the following explanation will dispense with some of the confusion.

During the 1930's the similar businesses of Shaw and Copestake Ltd. **(SylvaC Ware)** and Thomas Lawrence (Longton) Ltd. **(Falcon Ware)** worked closely together, due to family ties (and, later, acquisition of Thomas Lawrence Ltd. by Shaw and Copestake Ltd.) but each company was producing its own individual wares, in separate locations. However, during the Second World War years most of the Shaw and Copestake factory was requisitioned by the government, under the Concentration of Industries Scheme and production of the majority of their products was transferred to a part of the Thomas Lawrence factory, allocated to them for that purpose. In other words, Shaw and Copestake were producing their own products, under their own name, in the Falcon Ware factory, but when production of new models began there, which was a joint operation, a new batch of numbers was started. Presumably this was thought to be a good idea at the time and would indicate, or highlight, SylvaC pieces originating from the Thomas Lawrence/Falcon Ware factory, but that action has resulted in a nightmare for collectors in later years! Still, nobody was to know that at the time, of course!

When the Shaw and Copestake business was started in the 1890's their products were numbered, starting at no.1 (as far as can be established) and by the start of the Second World War were at something like no.1500. During the 1940's, and for a few years into the 1950's, the Shaw and Copestake products (SylvaC Ware) produced at the Thomas

Lawrence (Falcon Ware) factory were numbered 1 to 759, thus repeating numbers used much earlier at Shaw and Copestake's own factory.

In a nutshell, the original 1 to 759 numbers used by Shaw and Copestake at their own factory were stamped on pottery from circa 1894 to 1931. These pieces are generally known now as 'early SylvaC' or 'pre-SylvaC'. The duplicated 1 to 759 numbers, used on products (SylvaC) made in the Falcon Ware factory were stamped on pottery from circa 1940 to 1957. The two companies, though different in name, were virtually one, from the 1940's onwards, and many items made in the Falcon Ware factory had either 'SylvaC' **or** 'Falcon' on them - in some cases, **both** names were used on the same piece of pottery. By the time that the joint SylvaC production at the Falcon works eventually moved back to the Shaw and Copestake works in 1962 and Thomas Lawrence ceased trading, the 'new' numbering had been abandoned and absorbed into the ongoing and more logical Shaw and Copestake numbering. This numbering had reached something like 2400+ by then (don't forget, Shaw and Copestake were still continuing to produce their own products in their own right, within the Falcon factory and also they had limited production after the war in their own factory again) but just to add further to the confusion, for collectors now, Shaw and Copestake had allocated, to the Falcon factory, the numbers 3110-3183 (used mainly on animal models) circa 1947 to 1957! This particular move, however, should not really concern collectors as these numbers were Shaw and Copestake factory numbers anyway and were never duplicated.

To sum up, and explain it even more simply without all the detail, two sets of the numbers 1-759 were used - one set of 1-759 was used on Shaw and Copestake pottery from circa 1894 to 1931 and the other set of 1-759 was used on SylvaC pottery made at the Falcon Ware factory from circa 1940 to 1957. The majority of the earlier pottery will not have the name on it, the majority of the later pottery will - end of story!

4

Please read the following, in conjunction with the price guide:

The purpose of this book is to give a guide to the prices on the SylvaC items that were produced under **Falcon Ware factory numbering only**. These pieces are SylvaC just as much as all the other hundreds of pieces are and, because they have Falcon Ware factory numbering, does not mean that they are any the less collectable! On the following pages is an up-to-date listing of numbers 1 to 759 and against each mould number is a description (where known) of the item, followed by a suggested price. Underneath this information, **in brackets**, but using the same number, is a description of the item which has the earlier Shaw and Copestake numbering. Thus, the items against the mould number, and with the price guide, were first produced circa 1940 to 1957, whereas the bracketed items are circa 1900 to 1931. Obviously, there are many pieces of SylvaC which have never been seen, and which may never have been produced commercially, so a nominal price is given on those items, subject to more information coming to light.

N/I against the mould number indicates that there is no information known about that number. The price given covers all finishes but matt glaze pieces are likely to be more expensive than bright glaze examples, unless the bright glaze piece is rare anyway. As a general rule, animals are likely to be more expensive than items in other categories.

l/s = large size, **m/s** = medium size, **s/s** = small size, **sim** = similar to.

ACKNOWLEDGEMENTS

We would like to thank Susan Verbeek for information she gave us and for her kind permission in allowing us to use information from THE SYLVAC STORY, thereby making this publication possible. We would also like to thank the many members, past and present, of the SylvaC Collectors Circle who have given freely of their information and knowledge.

5

SylvaC - with Falcon factory numbers - Price Guide

No.	Description	Price
1	Deer, 6¼" high 6¼" long	£35-£50
	(N/I)	
2	N/I	
	(Vase, tall, two handles)	
3	Girl sitting on chair with doll, 6½" high	£55-£75
	(N/I)	
4	N/I	
	(N/I)	
5	N/I	
	(N/I)	
6	N/I	
	(N/I)	
7	N/I	
	(N/I)	
8	N/I	
	(N/I)	
9	Choir Boy, 6" high	£65-£85
	(N/I)	
10	N/I	
	(N/I)	
11	N/I	
	(N/I)	
12	N/I	
	(N/I)	
13	N/I	
	(N/I)	

No.	Description	Price
14	N/I	
	(N/I)	
15	Horse, standing, 6¾" high	£45-£60
	(N/I)	
16	Bulldog, standing, 5¼" high 8" long	£40-£65
	(Vase, narrow top, wider base, 11" high)	
17	Bison, 5" high 8" - 9" long 5. 6. 99	£45-£60 35·00
	(N/I)	
18	Spaniel, sitting, 5" high	£20-£45
19	Borzoi, lying, 4" high brown	£30-£50
	(Jug, sim 30, 11" high)	
20	Dog	£20-£45
	(N/I)	
21	Horse and Rider, 8½" high 9½" long	£75-£90
	(N/I)	
22	N/I	
	(N/I)	
23	N/I	
	(N/I)	
24	Bird wall plaque, possibly Kingfisher	£25-£40
	(N/I)	
25	Rabbit, holding skis, 3½" high	£35-£50
	(N/I)	
26	Rabbit, injured, 3" high	£35-£50
	(N/I)	

Handwritten annotations: alongside item 17 "35.00"; alongside item 18 "27-7-99 £38"; alongside item 19 "23·3·00 £50"; check marks next to items 17, 18, 19.

No.	Description	Price
27	Rabbit on skis, fallen down, 2¼" high	£35-£50
	(N/I)	
28	Rabbit on skis, 3¼" high	£35-£50
	(N/I)	
29	Rabbit on skis, 3" high	£35-£50
	(N/I)	
30	N/I	
	(Vase, narrow neck, ornate, partner to 19, 11" high)	
31	Dog on slipper, 6" long	£20-£35
	(N/I)	
32	N/I	
	(N/I)	
33	Lizard	£25-£40
	(N/I)	
34	Dog, sitting, begging, possibly Poodle, l/s	£35-£50
	(N/I)	
35	Scottie, standing, 1½" high 2¼" long	£25-£35
	(N/I)	
36	N/I	
	(Jug vase with narrow neck, 16" high)	
37	N/I	
	(N/I)	
38	N/I	
	(N/I)	
39	Red Riding Hood, 2" high	£25-£35
	(N/I)	

8

No.	Description	Price
40	Rhino, standing, 1¾" high	£25-£40
	(N/I)	
41	Elephant, standing, 1¾" high	£25-£40
	(N/I)	
42	Cat, sitting, smiling, tail up, 2" high	£25-£40
	(N/I)	
43	Duck Jug, 4¾" high	£40-£50
	(N/I)	
44	Rabbit Jug, 5" high	£30-£45
	(N/I)	
45	Dog Jug, 5" high *30·6·01 Beige*	£40-£50 *£41*
	(N/I)	
46	N/I	
	(N/I)	
47	Bulldog, sitting, 5" high	£30-£45
	(N/I)	
48	Rhino, standing, l/s	£40-£60
	(N/I)	
49	Lioness, head down, l/s	£40-£60
	(N/I)	
50	Camel, standing, l/s	£40-£60
	(N/I)	
51	N/I	
	(N/I)	
52	Bison, standing, 8¼" high 12" long	£50-£70
	(N/I)	

✓ (handwritten check mark next to No. 45)

No.	Description	Price
53	Bison, standing, head down, l/s	£50-£70
	(N/I)	
54	Eagle	£30-£50
	(N/I)	
55	Pony, standing	£25-£35
	(N/I)	
56	Buffalo, 5½" high 9½" long	£50-£70
	(N/I)	
57	St. Bernard, l/s	£30-£45
	(N/I)	
58	Lamp	£15-£30
	(N/I)	
59	Pelican, hunched up, sitting on rock, l/s	£50-£70
	(N/I)	
60	Horse, standing, short tail, l/s	£35-£45
	(N/I)	
61	N/I	
	(N/I)	
62	Lion, standing, l/s	£50-£70
	(N/I)	
63	Giraffe, standing, l/s	£50-£70
	(N/I)	
64	N/I	
	(N/I)	
65	N/I	
	(N/I)	

No.	Description	Price
66	Sea Lion, sitting on rock	£45-£65
	(N/I)	
67	Cairn Terrier, standing, 4" high	£25-£35
	(N/I)	
✓ 68	Elephant, standing, 9" high 14·7·01	£70-£95 £125
	(N/I)	
69	Bear, standing on hind legs, large	£45-£60
	(N/I)	
70	N/I	
	(N/I)	
71	Lamp - Eagle	£20-£40
	(N/I)	
72	Scottie, standing, 5¼" high 6½" long	£15-£40
	(N/I)	
✓ 73	Dog, sitting, with head cocked, 4¼" high	£20-£30
	(N/I)	
74	Gnome, sitting, holding toadstool, 6¾" high	£70-£95
	(N/I)	
75	Gnome, sitting, two pots each side, 6" high	£70-£95
	(Vase, small neck, fluted top, 9" high)	
76	N/I	
	(N/I)	
77	N/I	
	(N/I)	
78	N/I	
	(N/I)	

No.	Description	Price
79	N/I	
	(N/I)	
80	N/I	
	(N/I)	
81	Gnome, lying, with bowl, 8" long	£60-£80
	(N/I)	
82	Gnome, lying, resting, 8" long	£60-£80
	(N/I)	
83	Gnome, playing banjo by tree trunk, 8" high	£70-£90
	(N/I)	
84	Chimp/Monkey	£25-£40
	(N/I)	
85	Tiger, standing. (Also vase with floral pattern)	£25-£40
	(N/I)	
86	N/I	
	(N/I)	
87	Gnome, standing, by tree trunk, 7¼" high	£70-£90
	(N/I)	
88	Spaniel head wall plaque - 'Grouse', 3½" high	£35-£40
	(N/I)	
89	Scottie head wall plaque -'Mac', 4" high	£35-£45
	(N/I)	
90	Fox Terrier head wall plaque -'Bob', 3½" high	£35-£45
	(N/I)	
91	N/I	
	(N/I)	

No.	Description	Price	
✓ 92	Elephant, standing, 4" high *24.5.99*	£25-£35	*19.50*
	(N/I)		
93	Lion, lying, 2¼" high 6¾" long	£25-£40	
	(N/I)		
94	Bull, standing, head up, mouth open, 5¼" high	£30-£50	
	(N/I)		
95	Horse	£25-£35	
	(N/I)		
✓ 96	Chimpanzee, large, 7" high	£60-£80	*£50* *23-2-02*
	(N/I)		
✓ 97	Chimpanzee, small, arms folded, 4½" high	£25-£35	*£28* *23-2-02*
	(N/I)		
✓ 98	Chimpanzee, small, hand on right knee, 4" high	£25-£35	*25.12.01*
	(N/I)		
✓ 99	Cat, sitting, 5" high	£20-£35	*8.4.00* *£25*
	(N/I)		
✓ 100	Kitten, sitting, 2¾" high *12-3-99 BROWN 5-6-99 BLACK*	£15-£25	*26.40* *10.00*
	(N/I)		
✓ 101	Kitten, standing, 3" high 3¼" long *12.5.99*	£15-£25	*42.00*
	(N/I)		
✓ 102	Kitten, playing, 2¼" high 4" long *24.6.99*	£20-£30	*42.00*
	(N/I)		
✓ 103	Kitten, lying, 1¾" high 2¾" long *23.6.01*	£15-£25	*£20*
	(N/I)		
104	Cats in basket, 4¼" high	£25-£30	
	(N/I)		

No.	Description	Price
105	Mouse, crouching, large size, 3½" long	£30-£45
	(N/I)	
✓ 106	Mouse, sitting up, small size, 1½" high GREEN	£25-£40 13.10. 19-50 (A.F)
	(N/I)	
107	Foal, similar to 108/109, l/s, 12" high	£50-£75
	(N/I)	
108	Foal, standing, m/s, 8" high	£40-£60
	(N/I)	
108	Gnome, lying on his front, 10" high 14½" long	£70-£95
	--	
109	Foal, standing, s/s, 5½" high	£25-£35
	(N/I)	
109	Giraffe	£25-£40
	--	
110	Gnome, sitting on tree stump, 16" high	£80-£100
	(N/I)	
111	Girl	£30-£50
	(N/I)	
112	Boy	£30-£50
	(N/I)	
113	Gnome, lying against tree stump, 11" high 16" long	£80-£100
	(N/I)	
✓ 114	Spaniel, lying, 7" long 20.5.99	£20-£35 45.0
	(N/I)	
✓ 115	Spaniel Pup, sitting, 3" high 23.6.01	£15-£25 20.
✓	(N/I) " Bright Glaze 15.5.16	1.0

No.	Description	Price
✓ 116	Spaniel Pup, lying, 3¼" long 5·5·98	£15-£25 21·00
	(N/I)	
117	N/I	
	(N/I)	
118	N/I	
	(N/I)	
119	Cottage	£25-£40
	(N/I)	
120	N/I	
	(N/I)	
121	Candle holder	£15-£20
	(N/I)	
122	Bowl	£10-£20
	(N/I)	
123	Dish - Anenome, m/s, 8½" diameter	£25-£30
	(N/I)	
124	Horse, standing	£25-£40
'	(N/I)	
125	Horse	£25-£40
	(Plant pot, sim 127/404)	
126	Dish - Anenome, s/s, 7½" diameter	£20-£25
	(N/I)	
127	Dish - Anenome, l/s, 10¼" diameter	£30-£35
	(Jardiniere, large, sim 125/404, 7" high 9" diameter)	
128	Wall vase	£20-£35
	(N/I)	

No.	Description	Price
129	Posy hat, also with flowers, 4½" diameter (N/I)	£15-£25
130	Penguin, standing, l/s, 6" high (N/I)	£30-£35
131	Penguin, stooping, m/s, 4¼" high (N/I)	£25-£30
132	Penguin, standing, leaning forward, s/s, 4" high (N/I)	£25-£30
133	Penguin (N/I)	£25-£35
133	Hippo --	£25-£35
134	Bear, sitting up, 5½" high (N/I)	£25-£35
135	Horse, standing (N/I)	£25-£30
136	Tortoise trinket/cigarette box, 6½" long (N/I)	£120-£150
137	Bird (N/I)	£25-£35
138	Swallow (Vase, narrow top, wider base, 10¾" high)	£25-£35
139	Wall plaque, Swallow (Vase, narrow top, small base, 10½" high)	£30-£45
140	Horse, Cart Horse, standing, 4¾" high (N/I)	£20-£30

Handwritten note next to item 130: 18-8-04 £43.70

No.	Description	Price
141	Foal	£20-£30
	(N/I)	
142	Bear, standing, 2½" high	£30-£45
	(N/I)	
143	Flower holder	£10-£15
	(N/I)	
144	Flower holder	£10-£15
	(N/I)	
145	Scottie, standing, sometimes with tartan coat, 3½" h	£15-£30
	(N/I)	
146	Scottie Pup, playing, 2¼" high	£25-£35
	(N/I)	
147	Scottie Pup, standing, looking behind, 2¾" high	£25-£35
	(N/I)	
148	Scottie Pup, sitting, 2¾" high	£25-£35
	(N/I)	
149	Scottie, small, on chair	£25-£40
	(N/I)	
150	Rabbit holder	£15-£20
	(N/I)	
151	Posy holder, platform for animal or flowers, 1¼" high	£10-£15
	(N/I)	
152	Swan posy holder, also with china flowers, 3" high	£20-£40
	(N/I)	
153	Wall vase	£20-£30
	(N/I)	

Handwritten annotations: checkmarks beside 145 and 148; "30-11-02" and "£25" beside 148.

No.	Description	Price
154	Ashtray	£5-£15
	(N/I)	
155	Bulldog, standing, 3¼" high *Beige H.G'* *27.6.98* *13-1.18*	£25-£45
	(N/I)	
156	Wall vase	£20-£30
	(N/I)	
157	Dog, sitting, 3¾" high	£35-£50
	(N/I)	
158	Top hat, squashed, with dog and cat, 3" high	£20-£30
	(N/I)	
159	Elephant, cheerful, with fringed rug	£25-£40
	(N/I)	
160	Dog	£25-£40
	(N/I)	
161	Dog and basket weave bowl	£25-£40
	(N/I)	
162	Terrier, lying, 1¾" high 7½" long	£50-£00
	(N/I)	
163	Spaniel, sitting, 6" high	£40-£55
	(N/I)	
164	Manx cat, standing	£30-£40
	(N/I)	
165	Top hat, with kitten on rim, 3¼" high	£20-£30
	(N/I)	
166	Two Sealyhams joined, 3" high 6¼" long	£60-£80
	(N/I)	

No.	Description	Price
167	Horse	£25-£35
	(N/I)	
168	N/I	
	(N/I)	
169	Dish - shell with flowers, s/s	£10-£20
	(N/I)	
✓ 170	Poodle, sitting, 5¼" high 29·6·98	£25-£35 38-00
	(Vase with double handles)	
171	Container	£10-£15
	(N/I)	
172	Bear	£30-£40
	(N/I)	
173	Bear, playing, 1¾" high 2¾" long	£30-£40
	(N/I)	
174	Bear	£30-£40
	(N/I)	
175	Bear, standing, 3½" high 5¾" long	£35-£45
	(N/I)	
✓ 176	Boxer, standing, 4¾" high and (later) 5¼" high 22·12·98	£25-£45 14·50
	(Clock with pillars, 16" high)	
✓ 177	Dachshund, standing, 3" high 11·9·99	£25-£45 £14
	(N/I)	
178	Alsatian, lying, paws crossed, 4½" high	£25-£45
	(Spill vase, 4½" high)	
179	Spaniel puppy, sitting, sim 187	£30-£40
	(N/I)	

No.	Description	Price
180	Container	£10-£15
	(N/I)	
181	Top Hat	£10-£20
	(N/I)	
182	Boat	£15-£25
	(N/I)	
183	Donkey/Mule, sitting, laughing, 5½" high	£55-£70
	(Plant pot, 5" high 5" diameter)	
184	Vase, 14" high	£25-£35
	(N/I)	
184	Cat, boxing, 4¾" high	£55-£65
	--	
185	Alsatian Pup, sitting, 2¾" high (Also, Mermaid)	£25-£35
	(Jardiniere, 5" high 4¾" diameter)	
186	N/I	
	(N/I)	
187	Spaniel puppy, sitting sim 179	£30-£40
	(N/I)	
188	Vase, 12" high	£20-£30
	(N/I)	
188	Dachshund Pup, sitting, 1¾" high	£25-£35
	--	
189	Vase with two central circles (may be 681), 8¼" high	£10-£15
	(N/I)	
190	N/I	
	(N/I)	

TAN £
13-7-0L

No.	Description	Price
191	N/I	
	(N/I)	
192	Vase, slim shape	£10-£20
	(N/I)	
193	Vase, 10½" high	£15-£25
	(N/I)	
194	N/I	
	(N/I)	
195	N/I	
	(N/I)	
196	Ginger Jar with lid or as a vase, without lid, 7½" high	£20-£30
	(N/I)	
197	Ginger Jar with lid, 10¾" high	£25-£35
	(N/I)	
198	Plant pot, 5¾" high	£10-£15
	(N/I)	
199	Plant pot, 7" high	£15-£20
	(N/I)	
200	N/I	
	(N/I)	
201	Tray	£10-£15
	(N/I)	
202	Candle holder, tulip shape with handle, 2½" high	£20-£30
	(N/I)	
203	Setter, running, 4¼" high	£25-£35
	(N/I)	

No.	Description	Price
204	Scottie with collar, standing	£25-£40
	(N/I)	
205	Vase, 6¾" high	£10-£15
	(N/I)	
205	Foal	£20-£30
	--	
206	Vase, narrow top, s/s	£10-£15
	(N/I)	
206	Foal, lying, 1¾" high 4" long	£25-£35
	--	
207	Vase	£10-£20
	(N/I)	
207	Horse, Cart Horse, standing, 6" high	£25-£40
	--	
208	Horse	£25-£40
	(N/I)	
209	Boxer, sitting, 3½" high	£25-£40
	(N/I)	
210	Dachshund, on hind legs, begging, 6½" high	£25-£40
	(N/I)	
211	Dog	£25-£40
	(N/I)	
211	Jug	£15-£25
	--	
212	Yorkshire Terrier with bow, standing	£25-£40
	(N/I)	

TAN £20
13-7-02

22

No.	Description	Price
213	Foal	£25-£40
	(N/I)	
214	Shetland Pony, standing, 5" high	£25-£40
	(N/I)	
215	Vase, l/s	£20-£30
	(N/I)	
215	Spaniel, standing	£25-£40
	--	
216	Jug, sim 222, 5½" high	£15-£25
	(N/I)	
217	Jug, s/s	£15-£20
	(N/I)	
217	Dog	£25-£40
	--	
218	Jug, 5" high	£15-£25
	(N/I)	
219	Jug	£15-£25
	(N/I)	
220	Vase, narrow neck, l/s	£25-£30
	(N/I)	
221	Vase, 15" high	£25-£35
	(N/I)	
222	Jug, sim 216, 7" - 7½" high	£20-£35
	(N/I)	
223	Vase, 7½" high	£10-£25
	(N/I)	

No.	Description	Price
224	Vase, sim 226/228, 7½" high	£10-£20
	(N/I)	
225	Vase, 6½" high	£10-£20
	(N/I)	
226	Vase, sim 224/228, 6½" high	£10-£20
	(N/I)	
227	N/I	
	(N/I)	
228	Vase, sim 224/226, l/s	£15-£25
	(N/I)	
229	Vase	£10-£20
	(N/I)	
230	Vase with handles, l/s	£20-£30
	(Clock, very ornate, 11½" high 9" long)	
231	N/I	
	(N/I)	
232	N/I	
	(N/I)	
233	Vase with handles, 8" high	£20-£30
	(N/I)	
234	N/I	
	(N/I)	
235	N/I	
	(N/I)	
236	Vase, 8" high	£10-£20
	(N/I)	

No.	Description	Price
237	Vase, oval, 7" high	£10-£20
	(N/I)	
238	Vase, round, s/s	£10-£20
	(N/I)	
239	Vase with scalloped base, 8" high	£20-£30
	(N/I)	
240	Vase, diamond shape, 5¼" high	£15-£25
	(N/I)	
241	N/I	
	(N/I)	
242	N/I	
	(N/I)	
243	N/I	
	(N/I)	
244	Vase, raised flowers, 8" high	£20-£30
	(N/I)	
245	Jug, sim 222/216, 3½" high	£10-£15
	(N/I)	
246	Vase, curvy top, m/s	£20-£30
	(N/I)	
247	N/I	
	(N/I)	
248	Bowl on pedestal, Classic range, 4½" high 6¼" wide	£20-£30
	(N/I)	
249	Jug, 6¾" high	£20-£30
	(N/I)	

No.	Description	Price
250	N/I	
	(N/I)	
251	Bowl, sim 436	£15-£25
	(N/I)	
252	Bowl, 'Mandarin', 12" diameter	£25-£35
	(N/I)	
253	Bowl, 'Thorpe', 10" diameter	£20-£30
	(N/I)	
254	N/I	
	(N/I)	
255	Lamp base, same shape as 1807 vase	£25-£40
	(Vase, 13¾" high)	
256	Cucumber dish, Leaf Ware range, 10½" long	£15-£25
	(N/I)	
257	Vase, 'Collon'	£20-£30
	(N/I)	
258	Vase with two handles, 10" high	£20-£30
	(N/I)	
259	Jug, sim 260/272, 10" high	£25-£35
	(N/I)	
260	Jug, sim 259/272, 8" high	£20-£30
	(N/I)	
261	Jug to match 264, Leaf Ware range	£25-£35
	(N/I)	
262	Tray with handles, Spingbok range	£30-£40
	(Plant pot, 6¾" diameter), (Shaving mug)	

No.	Description	Price
263	N/I	
	(N/I)	
264	Beakers to match 261, Leaf Ware range	£5-£10
	(N/I)	
265	Vase	£10-£20
	(N/I)	
265	Tea Pot, Leaf Ware range, l/s	£15-£20
	--	
266	Honey pot, Springbok range	£20-£30
	(N/I)	
267	Cream jug, Springbok range	£20-£30
	(N/I)	
268	Covered sugar bowl, Springbok range	£20-£30
	(N/I)	
269	N/I	
	(N/I)	
270	N/I	
	(Vase)	
271	N/I	
	(N/I)	
272	Jug, sim 259/260, 12" high	£25-£35
	(N/I)	
273	Jug, sim 292/293, 12" high	£25-£35
	(Vase, 'Holborn', with handles, 9½" high)	
274	N/I	
	(N/I)	

No.	Description	Price
275	Vase, Springbok range (N/I)	£30-£40
276	Vase, Springbok range (N/I)	£30-£40
277	Bowl, Springbok range (N/I)	£25-£35
✓ 278	Hat posy ring, 10½" diameter 6.7.13 (N/I)	£25-£35 £7
279	Hat posy ring, 9" diameter (Vase, 11¾" high)	£20-£30
280	Hat posy ring, 6" diameter (N/I)	£15-£25
281	Hat flower pot, 8" across rim (Vase, sim 273, 11½" high)	£20-£30
282	Hat flower pot, 7½" across rim (N/I)	£15-£25
283	Hat flower pot, 6" across rim (Plant pot)	£15-£20
284	Tomato plate, Leaf Ware range (N/I)	£10-£20
285	Sweet dish, Leaf Ware range (N/I)	£10-£20
286	N/I (N/I)	
287	Bowl, on feet, 10" across (N/I)	£20-£30

No.	Description	Price
288	N/I	
	(N/I)	
289	N/I	
	(N/I)	
290	Sugar bowl, Leaf Ware	£10-£20
	(N/I)	
291	Vase	£10-£20
	(N/I)	
292	Jug, sim 273/293, 8" high	£20-£30
	(Vase, 9½" high)	
293	Jug, sim 202/273, 10" high	£25-£35
	(Vase with handles and curvy top, 11½" high)	
294	Candy box, Cavalier/Country Scenes, 5½" long	£10-£20
	(N/I)	
295	Toby jug, Cavalier	£20-£25
	(N/I)	
296	Mug	£15-£20
	(N/I)	
297	Twin tray, Hydrangea range, 9" long	£15-£25
	(N/I)	
298	Tray, Starglint range, 6½" diameter	£15-£25
	(N/I)	
299	Hat, nut basket, 7½" across	£25-£35
	(N/I)	
300	Jug, Cavalier/Country Scenes, 5¼" high	£20-£25
	(N/I)	

No.	Description	Price
301	Jug, Cavalier/Country Scenes, 4" high (N/I)	£15-£20
302	N/I (Plant pot, 8" high 10" diameter)	
303	N/I (Plant pot, sim 302, 7" high 8½" diameter)	
✓ 304	Jug, Cavalier/Country Scenes, 3" high (N/I)	£10-£20 *18.3.0* *£14*
305	Jug, Cavalier/Country Scenes, 2¼" high (N/I)	£10-£15
✓ 306	Cavalier character jug, new no.4487, 4¾" high (N/I)	£20-£30 *28.3.9* *£25*
307	Jug, Cavalier/Country Scenes, 4½" high (N/I)	£15-£25
308	Beaker, Cavalier, 4" high (N/I)	£10-£15
309	Jug, Cavalier/Country Scenes, 6¼" high (N/I)	£25-£40
310	Sugar bowl, Cavalier/Country Scenes, 3¼" dia. (Vase)	£5-£15
311	Straw hat (N/I)	£20-£30
312	Beefeater character jug, new no.4489, 4¼" high (N/I)	£15-£30
313	Jar, Cavalier (N/I)	£20-£30

No.	Description	Price
314	Hat cake basket, 10½" across	£30-£40
	(N/I)	
315	Posy bar, basket weave with ribbon, 6½" long	£5-£10
	(Plant pot on feet, 5¼" diameter)	
316	Vase	£10-£20
	(N/I)	
317	N/I	
	(N/I)	
318	Vase	£10-£20
	(N/I)	
319	Wall vase, incised diamond pattern, 7¼" high	£20-£30
	(N/I)	
320	Wall vase with gnomes, 7½" high *11·5-02*	£25-£40 *£50*
	(N/I)	
321	Wall vase, scalloped rim, 8" high	£25-£30
	(Vase, 9½" high)	
322	Jardiniere	£15-£20
	(N/I)	
323	Wall vase, toadstool with rabbit, 7¼" high *22-5-99*	£25-£40 *47.00*
	(N/I)	
324	N/I	
	(N/I)	
325	Teapot, Country Scenes	£15-£25
	(N/I)	
326	Sugar bowl, Country Scenes	£5-£10
	(N/I)	

No.	Description	Price
327	Wall plaque, boy whistling, with cap and scarf	£50-£65
	(N/I)	
328	Honey pot, Country Scenes	£10-£15
	(N/I)	
329	Wall plaque, girl's head, with scarf and kiss curl	£50-£65
	(N/I)	
330	Jug, Acorn with Squirrel handle, sim 1959	£30-£40
	(N/I)	
331	Teapot, Hydrangea range	£20-£30
	(N/I)	
332	Honey pot, Hydrangea range	£10-£15
	(N/I)	
333	N/I	
	(N/I)	
334	Jugs, sizes 1-4, Hydrangea range	£10-£35
	(N/I)	
335	Bowl, shallow, Country Scenes, 10" across	£15-£25
	(Vase with handles, 10" high)	
336	Jug, 10" high	£20-£30
	(Vase, sim 335, 7½" high)	
337	Triple tray, Hydrangea range	£20-£30
	(Vase, 12" high)	
338	Cream jug, Hydrangea range, s/s	£10-£15
	(Vase, sim 337, 13¼" high)	
339	Sugar bowl, Hydrangea range, s/s	£10-£15
	(N/I)	

No.	Description	Price
340	Plate, round, Country Scenes, l/s	£15-£25
	(N/I)	
341	Plate, round, Country Scenes, s/s	£10-£20
	(Plant pot, 6½" high 6" diameter)	
342	Cheese Dish, Hydrangea range	£25-£40
	(Vase set, sim 335, 7" and 6" high)	
343	Bowl, Hydrangea range, l/s	£20-£30
	(N/I)	
344	Jug, Hydrangea, sim 350/351, l/s	£25-£35
	(N/I)	
345	Coffee pot, Hydrangea range, l/s	£25-£35
	(Plant pot, two handles, three feet, sim 315, 4½" high)	
346	N/I	
	(N/I)	
347	Vase (unconfirmed)	£10-£20
	(Vase, two handles each side, 9½" high)	
348	Vase	£10-£20
	(N/I)	
349	Handbag Vase, 5½" high	£65-£85
	(N/I)	
350	Jug, Hydrangea, sim 344/351, s/s	£15-£25
	(Plant pot on four feet, 5" high)	
351	Jug, Hydrangea, sim 344/350, m/s	£20-£30
	(Clock)	
352	Mug, Hydrangea	£10-£15
	(N/I)	

No.	Description	Price
✓ 353	Log container with gnome, 8½" long 11·9·89 (N/I)	£20-£30 £15
✓ 354	Wall vase, tree with rabbit, 6" high 24·7·00 (Vase, sim 273 Holborn vase, 16" high)	£35-£45 £30
355	Tree jug with gnome or rabbit, 6¾" high (Vase on stand, sim 359, 6½" high)	£35-£45
356	N/I (N/I)	
357	N/I (Jardiniere, 4½" high 4½" diameter)	
358	Jug, embossed lines and ferns, 6½" high (N/I)	£15-£20
359	Fruit dish with two handles (Vase on stand, sim 355, 9¾" high)	£20-£30
360	Jug, herring-bone pattern, flowers, 5¾" high (Vase, sim 359, 12" high)	£20-£30
361	N/I (N/I)	
362	N/I (Plant pot on feet, 4½" high 4½" diameter)	
363	Jug, embossed band around centre, 9" high (Vase, sim 364/365, 7¼" high)	£35-£40
364	Jug, embossed flowers, rope handle, 6¼" high (Vase with handles, fluted top/base, 9½" high)	£20-£30
365	Sweet dish, Hydrangea range (Vase, sim 363/364, 12" high)	£10-£15

No.	Description	Price
366	Fruit dish, Hydrangea, s/s	£10-£15
	(Vase, sim 365, 12" high)	
367	N/I	
	(Vase, 10" high)	
368	Bulb bowl, embossed leaves, 7½" diameter	£15-£25
	(N/I)	
369	Fern pot, embossed leaves, 8" diameter	£15-£25
	(N/I)	
370	Vase, embossed leaves, 6¼" high	£15-£25
	(N/I)	
371	Jug, embossed flowers, leaves, 7¼"-8½" high	£20-£30
	(Vase with handles, 10" high)	
372	Tankard, Pickwick, 5" high	£25-£35
	(N/I)	
373	Tankard, Tavern in the Town, 5" high	£20-£30
	(N/I)	
374	Tankard, Old Bull and Bush, farmer's wife	£20-£30
	(Vase with handles, 11¾" high)	
375	N/I	
	(Vase, fluted handles, 12" high)	
376	Vase, 5½" high	£10-£25
	(Jardiniere, handles, sim 375, 7" high 12¾" wide)	
377	Drinking bowl, bird shape, 8" long	£25-£35
	(N/I)	
378	Drinking bowl, boat shape	£20-£30
	(N/I)	

No.	Description	Price
✓ 379	Drinking bowl, pipe shape　　　　11·9·99	£15-£20　£20
	(Vase)	
380	Vase, 8" high	£15-£30
	(Vase, sim 376, 5" high)	
381	Wall vase, ribbon	£25-£35
	(N/I)	
382	Wall vase, ribbon, 5" wide	£20-£25
	(N/I)	
383	Vase, top handle, 10" high	£15-£35
	(N/I)	
384	Galleon holder, 6¼" long	£20-£30
	(N/I)	
385	Vase, sim 387, no handles, 8¼" high	£15-£20
	(N/I)	
386	Jug, straight, 8" high	£15-£20
	(N/I)	
387	Vase, sim 385, with handles, 8¼" high	£15-£20
	(Vase with handles, 11½" high)	
388	N/I	
	(N/I)	
389	Bowl, twin horns	£25-£30
	(N/I)	
390	Dish with cover	£15-£20
	(N/I)	
391	Cigarette box	£15-£20
	(N/I)	

No.	Description	Price
392	Bowl	£15-£20
	(N/I)	
393	Cream jug, 3" high	£10-£15
	(N/I)	
394	Cream jug, 3" high	£10-£15
	(N/I)	
395	Jug, 3" high	£10-£15
	(N/I)	
396	Bowl	£15-£20
	(N/I)	
397	Jug, sim Crocus bud, 3"high	£15-£25
	(N/I)	
398	Jug, Rose, leaf handle, 3" high	£15-£25
	(N/I)	
399	Dish/tray with handles, 6½" diameter	£10-£15
	(Pot, embossed shells/scrolls, sim 401, 4½"high)	
400	Jug, Thistle, sim 683/730, 3" high	£15-£20
	(N/I)	
401	Jug, embossed leaves, 2¾" high	£15-£20
	(Plant pot, sim 399, 6¾" high)	
402	Jug	£15-£20
	(N/I)	
403	Coffee pot	£15-£20
	(N/I)	
404	Teapot	£15-£20
	(Plant pot, sim 125/127, 7" diameter)	

handwritten: 19-5-01 £10

handwritten: 24-7-99 £9-00

handwritten check mark next to 400

No.	Description	Price
405	Tray	£15-£20
	(N/I)	
406	Dorothy bag jug, sim 453, 7" high	£30-£45
	(N/I)	
407	Jug	£15-£20
	(N/I)	
408	Basket	£15-£20
	(N/I)	
409	Jardiniere, 10" long	£15-£35
	(N/I)	
410	Flower pot, s/s 3¾" h, m/s 4½" h, l/s 5¼" h	£10-£20
	(N/I)	
411	Flower pot, 4½" high, lattice pattern	£15-£20
	(Plant pot, 6¼" diameter)	
412	N/I	
	(Bowl, possibly with centrepiece, 11½" diameter)	
413	Bowl, Vine range, 12¼" long	£35-£45
	(N/I)	
414	Basket, Vine range, 10" long	£45-£60
	(N/I)	
415	Dish with handles, 11¼" long	£15-£25
	(Vase)	
416	Posy, leaf shape, also with butterfly, 7½" long	£15-£25
	(Vase, sim 418, 10"high)	
417	N/I	
	(Vase, sim 421)	

✓ 416 £10 13·8·0

No.	Description	Price
418	Bowl, 7¼" diameter	£15-£20
	(Vase, sim 416, 7½" high)	
419	Flower pot, Tulip, 4" high	£15-£20
	(Vase with handles, sim 425/445, 11½" high)	
420	Jug with petal base	£15-£20
	(Vase on square base, 11½" high)	
421	N/I	
	(Vase, oval, sim 446, 7½" high)	
422	N/I	
	(Vase, square base, narrow neck, 8½" high)	
423	Jug vase	£15-£20
	(N/I)	
424	Toastrack	£20-£25
	(Vase, sim 540)	
425	Bowl, hexagonal with three feet	£20-£30
	(Vase with handles, sim 419/445, 9½" high)	
426	Jug, sim 427, 6" high	£10-£20
	(Vase, 8½" high)	
427	Jug, sim 426, 9¼" high	£15-£25
	(N/I)	
428	Jardiniere	£15-£20
	(N/I)	
429	Log	£15-£20
	(N/I)	
430	N/I	
	(N/I)	

No.	Description	Price
431	Tray with Lizard, 7¼" long	£30-£40
	(Vase, sim 432, 8¼" high)	
432	Jug	£15-£20
	(Vase, 7½" high)	
433	Vase, also with Budgerigar, 8½" - 8¾" high	£10-£55
	(Clock, 5¼" high/ vases, 4½" high to match)	
434	Vase, 8¾" - 9" high	£15-£20
	(Vase)	
435	Vase, also with Budgerigar, 8¾" - 9" high	£10-£55
	(N/I)	
436	Bowl, 9½" diameter	£15-£20
	(Bowl, 9½" diameter, often with centrepiece)	
437	Bowl	£15-£20
	(N/I)	
438	N/I	
	(N/I)	
439	Vase	£10-£20
	(Vase, narrow neck, 7½" high)	
440	Vase	£10-£20
	(Rose bowl on pedestal, 6½" diameter)	
441	Jug	£15-£20
	(Rose bowl, 4" high 6½" wide)	
442	N/I	
	(N/I)	
443	Jardiniere with handles, ridges, 11" long	£15-£20
	(Vase, 6" high)	

No.	Description	Price
444	N/I	
	(N/I)	
445	Jardiniere, handles, embossed waves, 13½" long	£20-£30
	(Vase, sim 419/425, 8½" high)	
446	Tray	£15-£20
	(Vase, sim 421, 8½" high)	
447	Bowl	£15-£20
	(Rose bowl)	
448	N/I	
	(N/I)	
449	Fern pot	£15-£20
	(Vase with handles, 14" high)	
450	Butter/Cheese dish, tomato shape	£20-£30
	(N/I)	
451	N/I	
	(N/I)	
452	Posy curved, 7" long	£5-£10
	(N/I)	
453	Dorothy bag jug, sim 406, 3½" high	£15-£25
	(N/I)	
454	Posy	£5-£10
	(N/I)	
455	Jug, Dovecote range, 7¼" high	£35-£50
	(N/I)	
456	N/I	
	(N/I)	

No.	Description	Price
457	Jug, embossed 'Goulies and Ghosties', l/s (N/I)	£20-£30
458	Honey pot (N/I)	£10-£15
459	Table lamp, embossed leaves, 6¾" high (N/I)	£15-£25
460	Tray (N/I)	£15-£20
461	Flower jug, 7" high (N/I)	£20-£25
462	N/I (N/I)	
463	Jug, 5¾" high (N/I)	£15-£20
464	Jug with three spouts, 5" high (N/I)	£25-£35
465	Jug, Vine range, 8" high (N/I)	£50-£65
466	Jardiniere (N/I)	£15-£20
467	Jardiniere (N/I)	£15-£20
468	Bowl, round with frogs and lizards, l/s (N/I)	£30-£40
469	Bowl, sim 468, s/s, 3½" high (N/I)	£25-£35

No.	Description	Price
470	N/I	
	(N/I)	
471 ✓	Bowl, diamond, goes with 480/481, 10¼" across	£15-£25
	(N/I)	
472	Wall vase, Vine range, 8" high	£45-£55
	(N/I)	
473	Bowl, round, embossed, recess for owl, 7½" dia	£30-£40
	(N/I)	
474	Jardiniere with handles	£15-£20
	(N/I)	
475 ✓	Min. jug with Stork handle, sim 1960, 3" high	£15-£25
	(N/I)	
476	Min. jug, Hollyhocks, sim 1962, 3" high	£15-£25
	(N/I)	
477 ✓	Top hat, inverted with kitten on rim, 3¾" high	£20-£30
	(Flower holder, 3" high 7½" long)	
478	Jug, Vine range, 6" high	£50-£65
	(N/I)	
479	Bowl, embossed flowers, Sydney range, 12" across	£35-£45
	(N/I)	
480	Jug, diamond, goes with 471/481, 7" high	£20-£30
	(N/I)	
481	Posy bar, diamond, goes with 471/480, 8½" long	£10-£15
	(N/I)	
482	Tray (vase)	£15-£20
	(Clock, plain, 12" high)	

Handwritten annotations:
- Next to 471: 7-8-99 £15
- Next to 475: 31.7.99 18:00
- Next to 477: 16.12.98 23.40

No.	Description	Price
483	Vase	£10-£20
	(Spill vase, narrow middle, 4¾" high)	
484	Bowl, triangular, 10½" wide	£15-£25
	(Shaving/toothbrush mug, 4¼" high)	
485	Drinking bowl, higher one side, 5½" high	£15-£25
	(N/I)	
486	Jug, narrow, 10½" high	£20-£30
	(N/I)	
487	Jug, wavy serpent handle, 7¾" high	£20-£30
	(N/I)	
488	Bowl, wavy triangle, 4" high	£15-£25
	(N/I)	
489	Sauce boat, 12¾" long	£15-£20
	(Bowl, hexagonal, 3½" high 7¾" diameter)	
490	Jug, Sydney range, 8½" high	£30-£40
	(N/I)	
491	Sauce boat, 3½" high	£15-£20
	(N/I)	
492	N/I	
	(Rose bowl, 5¾" high 4½" wide)	
493	Bowl, two handles, 11½" long	£15-£20
	(Shaving mug, 4" high)	
494	Basket, two horns, 3¼" high	£25-£35
	(N/I)	
495	Settee	£25-£30
	(Vase, hexagonal with handles, sim 510, 11½" high)	

No.	Description	Price
496	Vase	£10-£20
	(Vase with handles, sim 509, 11½" high)	
497	Fruit dish, Dovecote range, 13" across	£30-£40
	(N/I)	
498	Bowl	£15-£20
	(N/I)	
499	Jug	£15-£20
	(N/I)	
500	Fruit bowl, Sydney range, 13½" across	£25-£35
	(N/I)	
501	Jug, Sydney range, 6" high	£25-£35
	(N/I)	
502	Bulb bowl, 4¾" high	£10-£15
	(N/I)	
503	Jardiniere/bulb bowl on four feet	£15-£20
	(N/I)	
504	Bowl	£15-£20
	(N/I)	
505	Bowl	£15-£20
	(N/I)	
506	Butter dish	£15-£20
	(N/I)	
507	Lamp	£20-£30
	(N/I)	
508	Bowl	£15-£20
	(N/I)	

No.	Description	Price
509	Basket, Shell range, 6½" high	£15-£25
	(Vase, sim 496, 10" high)	
510	Jug, Shell range, 9¼" high	£15-£20
	(Vase, sim 495, 9½" high, also Clock, small)	
511	Jug, Shell range, 6¼" high	£10-£15
	(Vase, sometimes with 510 clock, 11½" high)	
512	Jardiniere, Shell range, 14" long	£10-£20
	(N/I)	
513	Jardiniere, Shell range, 9¼" long	£10-£15
	(N/I)	
514	Jardiniere, Shell range, 6½" long 15.5.99	£10-£15 6.00
	(N/I)	
515	Vase	£10-£20
	(N/I)	
516	Onion face pot, 4" high 13-6-99	£10-£20 £11.00
	(N/I)	
517	Vase	£10-£20
	(N/I)	
518	Jug, narrow, 4¾" high	£10-£15
	(N/I)	
519	Bowl, Starglint range	£15-£20
	(N/I)	
520	Bowl with three holes	£15-£20
	(Clock, ornate, with pillars, 14" high 10½" wide)	
521	Hat	£15-£25
	(Vase with handles, 12" high)	

46

No.	Description	Price
522	N/I	
	(Vase, plain, upside down 'L' handles, 13¾" high)	
523	Wall vase	£20-£30
	(Dressing table tray)	
524	Wall vase, Sydney range, 8" high	£35-£45
	(N/I)	
525	Tray, oakleaf with acorn posy holder, 11½" long	£15-£20
	(N/I)	
526	Tray with leaf posy holder, 8½" long	£15-£20
	(N/I)	
527	Tray with cone posy holder, 8½" long	£15-£20
	(N/I)	
528	Tray with thistle posy holder, 13" long	£15-£20
	(Vase, 13" high)	
529	Butter dish, round, Dovecote range, 5" diameter	£20-£30
	(N/I)	
530	Cheese dish, Dovecote range, 4½" high	£30-£40
	(N/I)	
531	Fruit basket, Dovecote range, 11¼" across	£45-£55
	(N/I)	
532	Teapot, Dovecote range, similar to 577, l/s	£40-£50
	(N/I)	
533	Sugar bowl, Dovecote range, 3" diameter	£15-£20
	(Vase, for spills, 7" high)	
534	Cream jug, Dovecote range, 3¾" high	£15-£20
	(Vase, for spills, 8" high)	

No.	Description	Price
535	Honey pot, Dovecote range, 4" high	£15-£25
	(N/I)	
536	Cucumber dish, Dovecote range, 12½" long	£30-£40
	(N/I)	
537	N/I	
	(N/I)	
538	N/I	
	(Vase, sim 539/540/541/558/562, 7¾" high)	
539	N/I	
	(Vase, sim 538/540/541/558/562, 8½" high)	
540	Lettuce dish, Dovecote, (with stand), 8½" across	£40-£50
	(Vase, sim 538/539/541/558/562, 8" high)	
541	Salad bowl, Dovecote range, 9½" across	£40-£50
	(Vase, sim 538/539/540/558/562, 11½" high)	
542	Cup with plate (T.V.set), Dovecote range, 7¾" across	£15-£25
	(Tray, 'Napier', 13½" long 6" wide)	
543	N/I	
	(Vase, for spills, 6" high)	
544	Jug, also with Budgerigar, 9" high	£15-£85
	(N/I)	
545	Basket, also with Budgerigar, 8½" high	£25-£65
	(Vase, 6" high)	
546	Jardiniere, also with Budgerigar, 10" long	£15-£60
	(Vase, hexagonal, sim 548, 8½" high)	
547	Dish, shallow, also with Budgerigar, 13" across	£15-£55
	(N/I)	

No.	Description	Price
548	Jardiniere, Deco, also with Budgerigar, 9½" long	£20-£65
	(Vase, sim 546, with or without lid, 11¼"/17" high)	
549	Vase	£10-£20
	(N/I)	
550	Bowl, glacier, Penguin, goes with 572/591, 9¾" long	£35-£45
	(N/I)	
551	Jug, 10" high	£20-£25
	(N/I)	
552	Urn	£15-£20
	(N/I)	
553	Urn	£15-£20
	(Rose bowl, small)	
554	N/I	
	(N/I)	
555	N/I	
	(N/I)	
556	N/I	
	(Vase, sim 634, wider base, tall)	
557	Jug, Slymcraft range, 7" - 7¾" high	£10-£15
	(Bowl, wavy edges, 3" high)	
558	N/I	
	(Vase, sim 538/539/540/541/562)	
559	N/I	
	(Rose bowl, plated grid, 4½" - 5½" high, 7" diameter)	
560	Jug, embossed leaves and novelty, 6½" high	£25-£35
	(Jug, 8½" high)	

No.	Description	Price
561	Jug with tongue handle, 4½" high	£15-£25
	(Vase, 7½" high)	
562	Jug, Slymcraft range, 6½" high	£15-£20
	(Vase, sim 538/539/540/541/558, 14" high)	
563	N/I	
	(Jug, 6¾" and 7¾" high)	
564	Jug, 9" high	£20-£30
	(Vase, square handles, 12" high)	
565	Vase	£10-£20
	(Vase with handles, 11½" high)	
566	Vase, 10" high	£15-£25
	(Rose bowl, 5" diameter)	
567	Barrel with Duck, sim 569, 2½" high	£20-£30
	(Vase with handles, 11½" high)	
568	Bowl/novelty, 2½" - 2¾" high. Two versions 16/9/06	£20-£30	£8
	(N/I)	
569	Barrel with Duck, sim 567, 4¼" high	£25-£35
	(Bowl, Wild Duck range)	
570	Jug, narrow, 11" high	£20-£30
	(Vase, small handles, embossed band top, 8¼" high)	
571	Jug, wider centre, 8¾" - 9" high	£20-£30
	(N/I)	
572	Jug, glacier, Penguin, goes with 550/591, 8" high	£35-£45
	(N/I)	
573	Vase	£10-£20
	(Jugs, five sizes, 5", 5¼", 6", 7", 7¾" high)	

✓ 568

No.	Description	Price
574	N/I	
	(N/I)	
575	Vase	£10-£20
	(Rose bowl, two handles, 8½" high)	
576	Cup and Saucer, Dovecote, no number on items	£15-£20
	(Vase, square base, 11" high)	
577	Teapot, Dovecote range, sim 532, s/s	£35-£45
	(Vase)	
578	N/I	
	(Vase with handles, 6¾" high)	
579	Vase	£10-£20
	(N/I)	
580	Vase	£10-£20
	(Plant pot on four feet, 4" high)	
581	Basket	£20-£25
	(Vase, sim 582/583, 9¾" high)	
✓ 582	Orange honey pot, with lid, 3½" high 30·8·99	£15-£25 £18
	(Vase, ornate handles, sim 581/583, 11¾" high)	
✓ 583	Pineapple honey pot, with lid, 3½" high 12·8·99	£15-£25 £38
	(Vase, sim 581/582, 13¾" high)	
✓ 584	Grape honey pot, with lid, 3½" high (no lid) 19·5·16	£25-£35 50p
	(N/I)	
✓ 585	Strawberry honey pot, with lid, 3½" high 10·9·99.	£20-£30 26·55
	(Vase)	
586	Barrel with dog one end, 3" high	£25-£35
	(N/I)	

No.	Description	Price
587	Rabbit hutch container with rabbit, 8" long	£35-£45
	(Vase, ornate, with handles, 9½" high)	
588	Jug, as cone, with small Squirrel, l/s	£35-£45
	(N/I)	
589	Bowl, curved, 5" across	£15-£20
	(N/I)	
590	Bowl	£15-£20
	(N/I)	
591	Bowl, glacier, Penguin, goes with 550/572, 3¾ high	£30-£40
	(N/I)	
592	Bowl	£15-£20
	(N/I)	
593	N/I	
	(N/I)	
594	Penguin, probably for 591	£20-£30
	(Tray, Silvo range, 13½" long 6" wide)	
595	N/I	
	(N/I)	
596	Jug	£15-£20
	(N/I)	
597	Bowl	£15-£20
	(N/I)	
598	Bulb bowl	£15-£20
	(N/I)	
599	Vase	£10-£20
	(N/I)	

No.	Description	Price
600	Vase	£10-£20
	(Vase, sim 610/611, 9¾" high)	
601	Vase	£10-£20
	(Plant pot, sim 602/603, 5" high)	
602	Vase	£10-£20
	(Plant pot sim 601/603, 6" diameter)	
603	Urn vase, Lion handles, 10¼" high	£20-£30
	(Plant pot, sim 601/602, 7" diameter)	
604	Urn vase, Lion handles, 8½" high	£15-£25
	(Clock, 12" high)	
605	Bowl	£15-£20
	(Clock, heart shape, 9¼" high)	
606	Jug	£15-£20
	(Vase, heart shape, partner to 605, 7¼" high)	
607	Vase	£10-£20
	(N/I)	
608	Scorpion	£25-£35
	(Clock, heart shape, round/square centre, 11½" high)	
609	Punch bowl, embossed edge, 6¼" high 10" diameter	£25-£35
	(Vase, partner to 608, 9½" high)	
610	N/I	
	(Vase, sim 600/611, 7¾" high)	
611	N/I	
	(Vase, sim 600/610, 11½" high)	
612	N/I	
	(N/I)	

No.	Description	Price
613	N/I	
	(Vase, 8" high)	
614	Shell bowl, 7" across	£10-£15
	(Vase, 9¼" high)	
615	Jardiniere Sea Shell range, sim 616/618, 5¾" long	£5-£10
	(N/I)	
616	Jardiniere, Sea Shell range, sim 615/618 9½" long	£15-£20
	(N/I)	
617	Flower pot, Sea Shell range, 5" high	£10-£15
	(N/I)	
618	Jardiniere, Sea Shell range, sim 615/616, 7¾" long	£15-£20
	(N/I)	
✓ 619	Butter dish with Cow on lid, 5" long 11 ૧·૧૧	£15-£25 £4
	(N/I)	
620	Butter pot, round, with Cow on lid	£15-£25
	(Tray and also Flower pot, 6¼" high)	
✓ 621	Stilton cheese dish, Mouse on lid, round, 6¾" dia	£20-£30 4·3 2ul £40
	(Vase, 13½" high)	
622	Vase, angular hour glass shape, 7" high	£20-£30
	(Vase, 14" high)	
623	Vase, 7" high	£20-£30
	(N/I)	
624	Vase, three tiered, 7" high	£20-£30
	(N/I)	
625	Vase, fish shape, 7¼" high	£20-£30
	(N/I)	

No.	Description	Price
626	Vase, cone shape, 7¼" high	£15-£20
	(Vase, sim 627, 7¾" high)	
627	Bowl on pedestal, Classic range	£15-£20
	(Vase, sim 626, 10" high)	
628	Vase, Classic range, 8" high	£10-£20
	(N/I)	
629	Vase, Classic range, 9" high	£15-£20
	(Vase, sim 614, 11½" high)	
630	Vase, Classic range, 6" high	£10--£15
	(Clock, 14" high)	
631	Bowl, Classic range, 6" across	£10-£15
	(Bowl, round, three feet, 7" diameter)	
632	Vase, Classic range, 10" high	£15-£20
	(N/I)	
633	N/I	
	(N/I)	
634	Bowl	£15-£20
	(Vase for spills, 6" high)	
635	Bowl	£15-£20
	(Vase for spills, seen with silver rim, 4" - 5" high)	
636	Bowl, 10¾" long	£10-£15
	(Vase for spills, sim 634, 8" high)	
637	N/I	
	(Vase, 12" high)	
638	Bowl on feet	£15-£20
	(N/I)	

No.	Description	Price
639	Bowl	£10-£15
	(N/I)	
640	Jardiniere, Handkerchief range, 8½" high	£15-£20
	(Tray)	
641	Vase, Handkerchief range, 8½" high	£15-£20
	(N/I)	
642	Bowl, Handkerchief range, 11¾" long	£15-£20
	(Shaving mug, 3¼" high 6" long)	
643	Bowl, Handkerchief range, 10¼" long	£15-£20
	(Cheese dish, oblong, base 7½" long)	
644	Vase, Handkerchief range, 7" high	£15-£20
	(N/I)	
645	Wall vase, Classic range, 9" high	£15-£25
	(Clock, 11½" high)	
646	Flower pot, Classic range, 5" high	£10-£15
	(N/I)	
647	Flower pot, Classic range, 4" high	£10-£15
	(N/I)	
648	Jardiniere, Classic range, 10" long	£15-£20
	(Vase, Gothic, 10½" high, also Clock, 11½" high)	
649	Bowl, Classic range, 8½" across	£15-£20
	(Clock, plain, oval/ round face, / Wild Duck, 10" h)	
650	Vase, two entwined, 6" high 24-7-99 5.6.99	£20-£30
	(Vase, plain or embossed to match 649, 7½" high)	
651	Vase	£10-£20
	(Clock, partners 652, 11¼" long)	

(handwritten notes near row 650: £13·00, 81·00 (Pair))

56

No.	Description	Price
652	Jardiniere, Handkerchief range, 7" high	£15-£20
	(Vase, partners 651, 8½" high)	
653	Wall vase, Handkerchief range, 8" high	£20-£25
	(Vase with silver rim, 5" high)	
654	Tray	£15-£20
	(Sandwich tray, matching unnumbered plates, 12½"l)	
655	Vase, Cactus shape, 7" high	£15-£20
	(N/I)	
656	Vase, vertical ridges, Cactus-like	£15-£20
	(N/I)	
657	Bowl	£15-£20
	(N/I)	
658	Vase	£10-£20
	(N/I)	
659	Wall vase	£20-£25
	(Vase, plain, 9½" high)	
660	N/I	
	(N/I)	
661	N/I	
	(N/I)	
662	N/I	
	(N/I)	
663	Bowl	£15-£20
	(Vase, embossed chinese scene, sim 703, 12" high)	
664	N/I	
	(N/I)	

No.	Description	Price
665	N/I	
	(N/I)	
666	Candle holder	£10-£15
	(Jugs, octagonal, 6¾", 7½" and 8¾" high)	
667	Candle holder, 4¼" high	£10-£15
	(N/I)	
668	Wall vase with handle	£25-£35
	(N/I)	
669	Candle holder	£10-£15
	(Vase, sim 696, 11" high)	
670	Candle holder	£10-£15
	(N/I)	
671	N/I	
	(N/I)	
672	Candy box	£10-£15
	(N/I)	
673	Dish, shallow	£10-£15
	(N/I)	
674	Vase, 5" high	£10-£15
	(Plate, oval)	
675	Vase with swirls, sim 1571, 5" high	£10-£15
	(Wall plaque, 11¾" long, 8" wide)	
676	Vase, sim 1562/1563/1564, 5" high	£10-£15
	(N/I)	
677	Vase	£10-£15
	(N/I)	

Handwritten annotations: "✓" beside 674 and 675; "1.4.09" and "£--" beside 674; "18.3." and "£6" beside 675.

No.	Description	Price
678	Vase, opening to cone shape, 6" high	£10-£15
	(Vase, sim 679, 10" high)	
679	Vase, plain cone shape, 6" high	£10-£15
	(Vase, sim 678, ornate handles, 11" high)	
680	N/I	
	(Bowl, wavy, embossed, 2½" high, with bird centre)	
681	Vase, two central circles (could be 189)	£10-£15
	(N/I)	
682	Vase, unsymmetrical 'handles', 6" high	£10-£15
	(Clock, sim 783 but larger)	
683	Vase, 'Thistle', sim 400/730, 6" high	£15-£20
	(Butter/Cheese dish, 3" high)	
✓ 684	Vase, sim 1343, 5" high	£10-£15 21-8-99 £6
	(N/I)	
685	N/I	
	(N/I)	
686	Basket, wicker pattern, 10½" high, approx.	£20-£30
	(N/I)	
687	Wall vase, Coconut with Blue-Tit, 6½" high	£35-£45
	(N/I)	
✓ 688	Tree trunk vase with Blue-Tit, 7" high	£25-£35 22-7-00 £50
	(N/I)	
✓ 689	Tree trunk triple vase with Blue-Tits, 6" high	£30-£40 7-8-99 £40
	(Plant pot, 'Lord & Lady', 4½" high)	
690	N/I	
	(Plant pot, 'Lord & Lady', 5½" high)	

No.	Description	Price
691	N/I	
	(N/I)	
692	N/I	
	(N/I)	
693	N/I	
	(Plant pot, 'Lord & Lady', l/s)	
694	N/I	
	(Clock, 'Lord & Lady'/Vase, 5½" high/Tray 1¾" h)	
695	Bowl	£15-£20
	(Clock set, 'Lord & Lady', clock/vases 8" high)	
696	N/I	
	(Clock, 'Lord & Lady', 9¾" high/Vase, 8½" high)	
697	Hand holding vase, 5" high	£10-£15
	(Vase, 'Lord & Lady', handles, sim 699, 11" high)	
698	Pot	£10-£15
	(Vase, 'Lord & Lady', 9¾" high)	
699	Candle holder/pot	£10-£15
	(Vase, 'Lord & Lady', handles, sim 697, 11½" high)	
700	Kingfisher (using S. & C. number), 6½" high	£20-£30
	(Kingfisher, to go with various bowls, 6½" high)	
701	Bowl	£15-£20
	(Swallow)	
702	Bowl, usually with Golden Crested Grebe, 11" acr.	£35-£45
	(N/I)	
703	Barrel/barrow	£10-£15
	(Vase, Chinese scene, sim 663, 10" high)	

No.	Description	Price
704	Jug	£15-£20
	(Plant pot, 'Lord & Lady', sim 714/715, 4¾" high)	
705	Bowl	£15-£20
	(Vase, 'Lord & Lady', 9¾" high)	
706	Bowl	£15-£20
	(N/I)	
707	Lazy pixie, etc., novelty toadstool, 3" high 4·9·99	£20-£30 £15
	(N/I)	
708	Lazy pixie/floral, novelty wheelbarrow, 5" long	£20-£30 £29-70
	(N/I)	
709	N/I	
	(Pair vases, embossed, each different scene, 10" high)	
710	Vase, fish balancing on tail, goes with 725, 8" high	£15-£20
	(N/I)	
711	Vase	£10-£20
	(Bowl, embossed flowers, goes with 700, 3" high)	
712	Vase	£10-£20
	(N/I)	
713	Wall vase	£15-£20
	(N/I)	
714	Jardiniere	£15-£20
	(Plant pot, 'Lord & Lady', sim 704/715, 6" high)	
715	N/I	
	(Plant pot, 'Lord & Lady', sim 704/714, 7½" high)	
716	Flower jug	£15-£20
	(Jardiniere, 'Lord & Lady', 11" diameter)	

No.	Description	Price
717	Tray	£15-£20
	(N/I)	
718	Wall vase, 12½" across	£20-£25
	(Plant pot, 'Lord & Lady', straight sides, 6¼" high)	
719	Tray	£15-£20
	(N/I)	
720	Hat	£15-£20
	(N/I)	
721	Cap wall vase, 4½" high	£20-£25
	(N/I)	
722	Hat	£15-£20
	(Bowl, octagonal, embossed fairies, 11" diameter)	
723	Hat	£15-£20
	(N/I)	
724	Shell bowl, Nautilus range, 9" across	£15-£20
	(N/I)	
725	Vase, fish balancing on head, goes with 710, 9½" h	£15-£20
	(N/I)	
726	Wall vase, Nautilus range, 8" high	£20-£30
	(Bowl, embossed garden scene, with 700, 2½" high)	
727	Dish, triangular, small	£10-£15
	(Twin vase, 'Sydney Harbour Bridge', 8½" long)	
728	N/I	
	(Bowl/Vase, 'Lord & Lady', 6" high)	
729	Vase	£10-£20
	(N/I)	

No.	Description	Price
730	Vase, 'Thistle', sim 400/683, 10" high	£20-£30
	(N/I)	
731	Vase, 'studs' down side, 9" high	£15-£20
	(N/I)	
732	Trilby hat wall vase, 4¾" high	£30-£45
	(N/I)	
733	Boater hat wall vase, 4¾" high	£30-£45
	(Pelican in top hat, beside posy holder, 8" high)	
734	Vase, similar to 751/752, 8" high	£10-£20
	(N/I)	
735	Cactus in pot, 5" high	£30-£40
	(N/I)	
736	Cactus in pot, 5" high	£30-£40
	(N/I)	
737	Cactus in pot, 5" high	£30-£40
	(N/I)	
738	Cactus in pot, 5" high	£30-£40
	(N/I)	
739	Vase, sim 748/749, 8" - 8¼" high	£10-£20
	(N/I)	
740	Vase	£10-£20
	(N/I)	
741	Vase, sim 2337/2352, 8¼" - 8½" high	£10-£20
	(N/I)	
742	Cactus in pot, 3" high	£30-£40
	(N/I)	

No.	Description	Price
743	N/I	
	(Airedale, also with vase, 7"high 9"long)	
744	Vase, uneven top, 5" high	£10-£15
	(Clock with handles, 10½" high 10" wide)	
745	Vase, top opens out, 5" high	£10-£15
	(N/I)	
746	Vase, studded surface, 5" high	£10-£15
	(N/I)	
747	Wheelbarrow, usually with pixie, l/s, 10½" long	£15-£60
	(Bowl, embossed, with Monkey centrepiece)	
748	Vase, sim 739/749, 10¼" high	£15-£20
	(N/I)	
749	Vase, sim 739/748, 6" high	£10-£15
	(Vase, 6" high)	
750	Vase	£10-£20
	(N/I)	
751	Vase, sim 734/752, 6" high	£10-£15
	(Dog)	
752	Vase, sim 734/751, 10½" high	£15-£20
	(Pekinese, standing, 6½" high 7½" long)	
753	Jardiniere, Nautilus range, 7½" high	£15-£25
	(N/I)	
754	Jug	£15-£20
	(N/I)	
755	Vase	£10-£20
	(N/I)	

handwritten note next to 747: 31.7.9 £15

No.	Description	Price
756	Jardiniere, Nautilus range, 9½" high	£25-£30
	(N/I)	
757	N/I	
	(Plant holder, Wild Duck, sim 812, l/s)	
758	N/I	
	(N/I)	
759	N/I	
	(Shell jardiniere)	

There were many other SylvaC-marked items made at the Falcon Ware factory during this period but which were either not allocated numbers or did not have the numbers shown on them. Examples of this include The Wishing Well range, the Roma Basket, the Lucknow Lamp, the Crescent Basket, the Crescent Boat and a number of named vases - the 'Chang No.1', the 'York', etc. Often, individual vases, jugs, bowls, etc. were finished in a variety of different decorations and designs and were used in several different ranges, with the same basic shape number, or mould number, remaining the same - the price banding is designed to accommodate all these variations.

ILLUSTRATION CROSS REFERENCE

Illustrations of a considerable number of the pieces listed in the price guide can be found in other SylvaC publications. To further assist in the identification of a particular item, check for its number in the listings on the following pages. Against the number is the name of the publication the piece appears in, followed by the page number on which it appears. There are two separate listings, one for the Falcon Ware factory numbers and one for the earlier Shaw and Copestake numbers. **TSS** = The SylvaC Story by Susan Jean Verbeek, **TSC** = The SylvaC Companion by Susan Jean Verbeek, **CS** = Collecting SylvaC by Mick and Derry Collins, **CGES** = Shaw & Copestake - The Collectors Guide to Early SylvaC by Anthony Van Der Woerd.

FALCON WARE FACTORY NUMBERS

No.	Book	Page	No.	Book	Page	No.	Book	Page
15	TSS	48	96	TSC	31	170	TSS	41
15	CS	45	97	TSS	47	176	TSS	42
15	TSC	106	97	TSC	31	177	TSS	42,43
16	TSS	48	98	TSS	47	178	TSS	43
16	TSC	22	98	CS	40	183	TSS	50
18	TSS	41,42	98	TSC	31	183	CS	46
18	CS	45	99	TSS	47	184	TSS	50,84
18	TSC	19	99	CS	40	184	CS	46
21	TSS	85	100	TSS	47	185	TSS	43
25	TSS	37	101	TSS	47	188	TSS	42,43
26	TSS	37	102	TSS	47,84	192	TSC	138
27	TSS	37	103	TSS	47	196	TSC	67,102
28	TSS	37	104	TSS	84	196	TSC	144
29	TSS	37	106	CS	41	197	TSC	67
31	TSS	38	107	TSS	50	198	TSC	67
43	CS	38	108	TSS	52	199	TSC	67
43	TSC	137	110	TSS	52	203	TSS	42
44	TSC	137	113	TSC	124	207	TSS	48
45	TSC	137	114	TSS	41,42	209	TSS	42
68	TSS	47	115	TSS	41,42	210	TSS	42
68	TSC	31	116	TSS	41,42	214	TSS	?
72	TSS	103	129	TSS	31	216	TSS	97
73	TSS	106	134	TSC	30	216	TSC	138
74	TSC	124	136	TSS	37	218	TSC	147
75	TSC	124	136	CS	45	221	TSC	138,144
81	TSC	124	145	TSS	41	222	TSS	97
82	TSS	52	146	TSS	41	222	TSC	138
83	TSS	52	147	TSS	41	223	TSC	67
87	TSS	52	148	TSS	41	225	TSC	138
88	CS	45	152	TSS	31	226	TSC	138,147
92	TSS	47	155	TSS	41	228	TSC	138
92	CS	40	166	CS	46	230	TSC	138
92	TSC	31	166	TSC	23	233	TSC	138
96	TSS	47	169	TSS	36	236	TSC	138,145

No.	Book	Page	No.	Book	Page	No.	Book	Page
237	TSC	138	307	TSS	35	380	TSC	102,144
238	TSC	138	307	TSC	151	383	TSC	103
239	TSC	138	306	TSS	35,88	384	TSS	37
240	TSC	138	309	TSC	151	385	TSC	102
246	TSC	147	310	TSC	151	386	TSC	101
249	TSC	67	312	TSS	35	387	TSC	103
252	TSC	105,144	312	TSC	126	393	TSC	101
252	TSC	145	320	TSS	54	394	TSC	101
253	TSC	145	323	TSS	54	398	CS	38
258	TSC	103	325	TSC	151	399	TSC	147
259	TSC	67,101	328	TSC	151	400	TSS	66
259	TSC	144	330	TSC	112	406	TSS	57
260	TSC	101,144	331	TSC	141	409	TSC	92,104
262	TSC	47	332	TSC	141	409	CS	37
266	TSC	47	334	TSC	140	410	TSS	53
267	TSC	47	335	TSC	151	418	TSC	142
268	TSC	47	337	TSC	140	426	TSC	101,102
272	TSC	101,144	338	TSC	141	427	TSC	101,102
273	TSC	145	339	TSC	141	431	TSS	37
275	TSC	47	340	TSC	151	436	TSS	54
276	TSC	47	341	TSC	151	455	TSS	57
277	TSC	47	342	TSC	140	455	TSC	148
282	TSS	86	343	TSC	140	463	TSC	102
287	TSC	105	344	TSC	140	465	TSC	148
292	TSC	145	345	TSC	141	468	TSS	57
293	TSC	145	349	CS	47	469	TSS	86
294	TSC	151	350	TSC	140	471	TSS	53
297	TSC	140	351	TSC	140	473	TSS	86
300	TSS	35	353	TSS	53,86	475	TSS	66
300	TSC	151	354	TSS	54	475	CS	47
304	TSS	35	355	TSS	57,86	476	TSS	66
304	TSC	151	365	TSC	140	479	TSC	143
305	TSS	35	366	TSC	140	485	TSC	105
305	TSC	151	368	TSC	142	486	TSC	102
305	CS	38	376	TSC	147	489	TSC	72

No.	Book	Page	No.	Book	Page	No.	Book	Page
490	TSC	143	569	TSS	86	675	TSC	94,103
493	TSC	105	571	TSC	102	676	TSC	94
494	TSC	105	572	TSS	86	679	TSS	85
497	TSS	86	582	TSS	59,86	684	TSC	94,103
500	TSC	143	583	TSS	59,86	689	TSS	86
501	TSC	143	585	TSS	59,86	697	TSS	31
509	TSC	66	585	CS	37	700	TSS	54,96
510	TSC	66	586	TSS	38	700	CS	27
511	TSC	66	586	CS	35	702	TSS	54
512	TSC	66	587	TSS	86	707	TSS	32,54
513	TSC	66	591	TSS	53,86	707	TSC	112
514	TSC	66	599	TSC	72	708	TSS	31
516	TSS	59	603	TSC	92	710	TSC	90
524	TSC	143	615	TSC	92	711	TSC	72
530	TSC	148	616	TSC	92	712	TSC	72
535	TSS	86	618	TSC	92	713	TSC	72
536	TSC	148	619	TSS	59	714	TSC	72
544	TSS	14	621	TSS	59	716	TSC	72
544	CS	47	623	TSC	103	718	TSC	73,90
545	TSS	14	626	TSC	102	721	TSS	54
545	CS	47	628	TSC	91,94	724	TSC	70
546	TSC	72,73	629	TSC	91	725	TSC	90
546	TSC	92	630	TSC	91	726	TSC	70
548	TSS	86	631	TSC	91	727	TSC	72
549	TSC	72	632	TSC	91	732	TSS	54
550	TSS	86	636	TSC	72,73	733	TSS	54
557	TSC	76,102	639	TSC	72	736	TSS	54
561	TSC	101	645	TSC	91	739	TSC	73
561	CS	38	646	TSC	91	741	TSC	73
562	TSC	101	648	TSC	91	747	TSS	53
564	TSC	102	649	TSC	91	749	TSC	73
566	TSC	102	656	TSC	90	753	TSC	70,73
567	TSS	61	673	TSC	72	756	TSC	70
568	TSS	61	674	TSC	94			

SHAW AND COPESTAKE NUMBERS

No.	Book	Page	No.	Book	Page	No.	Book	Page
19	TSS	98	371	TSS	81	511	CGES	41,50
30	TSS	98	371	CGES	40	520	CGES	50
36	TSS	20	374	TSC	35	523	CGES	44
75	CGES	38	374	CGES	41	538	CGES	43
75	CS	22	375	CGES	39	539	CGES	41
127	TSC	36	376	CGES	39	540	TSS	95
127	CGES	58	387	CGES	37	540	CS	24
127	CS	22	416	CGES	39	548	CGES	40
183	CS	23	419	TSC	35	559	TSS	97
185	CGES	59	419	CGES	37,42	559	CGES	57
230	CGES	52	419	CS	24	560	TSC	38
230	CS	23	420	CGES	38	560	CGES	61
255	CGES	41	421	TSC	35	562	CGES	36,40
262	CGES	58,59	422	CGES	37	563	CGES	60
273	TSS	20	425	TSC	35	565	CGES	35
273	TSC	35	426	CGES	43	570	CGES	43
273	CGES	42	432	TSS	81	573	TSS	83
279	CGES	36	432	CGES	43	573	TSC	38
281	CGES	37	433	CGES	43,51	573	CGES	61
302	CGES	58	433	CGES	55	573	CS	25
315	CGES	59	436	TSS	54,96	575	TSC	35
321	CGES	42	436	CGES	73	575	CGES	57
337	TSC	35	440	CGES	57	578	TSS	81
338	CGES	41	445	CGES	38,40	578	TSC	35
347	CGES	42	446	CGES	37	582	CGES	38
354	CGES	34	449	CGES	38	587	CGES	40
354	CS	23	482	CGES	53	594	CGES	44
355	CGES	43	484	CGES	48	600	TSC	35
357	CGES	39	489	CGES	80	600	CGES	42
359	CGES	42	492	CGES	57	600	CS	25
363	CGES	59	496	CGES	37	603	CGES	58
363	CS	33	509	TSS	81	604	TSC	37
365	CGES	41	510	CGES	38	604	CGES	53

No.	Book	Page	No.	Book	Page	No.	Book	Page
605	TSS	82,83	649	TSS	83	703	CGES	65
605	CGES	50	649	CGES	51,54	704	TSC	37
606	TSS	82	650	TSS	83	709	TSS	107
606	TSC	42	650	CGES	51,54	711	TSS	96
606	CGES	50	650	CGES	56	714	TSS	96
606	CS	33	651	CGES	53	715	TSS	96
608	CGES	49	654	CGES	57	718	TSS	96
609	CGES	49	659	CGES	56	722	TSS	96
610	CGES	43,52	666	CGES	61,62	726	TSS	96
610	CS	26	675	CGES	57	726	CGES	73
611	CGES	28	679	CGES	42	727	TSS	96
614	TSC	42	680	TSS	96	728	TSS	96
614	CS	33	693	TSS	96	733	CGES	73
626	CGES	51	694	CS	26	743	TSC	37
627	CGES	36	696	CGES	55	743	CGES	73
629	CGES	37	698	TSS	96	743	CS	27
634	CGES	43	700	TSS	54,96	744	CGES	52
636	CGES	43	700	CGES	73	752	CGES	73
643	CGES	62	700	CS	27			
648	CGES	49	703	TSS	109			

IN RESPECT OF CURRENT PRICES FOR THE WHOLE OF THE SHAW
AND COPESTAKE FACTORY PRODUCTION ONLY, PLEASE REFER
TO THE FOLLOWING:-

The SylvaC Collectors Handbook - Part 1, by Anthony Van Der Woerd.
This book lists the prices for mould numbers 1 to 3000 only.

The SylvaC Collectors Handbook - Part 2 , Second Edition, by Anthony
Van Der Woerd.
This book lists the prices for mould numbers 3001 to the last recorded item,
number 6128.

"FALCON"
Ware

by

THOS. LAWRENCE
(LONGTON) LTD.

**FALCON WORKS
LONGTON
STOKE-ON-TRENT**

"SYLVAC"
Ware

by

SHAW &
COPESTAKE LTD.

**SYLVAN WORKS
LONGTON
STOKE-ON-TRENT**